Library of Congress Control Number: #2017908100
www.ericapooler.com

This book is dedicated to every child that has been labeled as "at-risk," I challenge you to rip off that label and replace it with one that depicts what you can and will do in your life.

Don't wait for someone else to raise your bar of expectations. You are not at-risk, you are at-potential!

Dr. Erica Pooler

The United States labels you as "At-Risk." According to Education Reform, the term at-risk is often used to describe students or groups of students who are considered to have a higher probability of failure academically. At-risk students have a higher rate of high school drop outs. The term may be applied to students who face circumstances that could jeopardize their ability to complete school, such as homelessness, incarceration, teenage pregnancy, serious health issues, domestic violence, transiency, or other conditions. It also refers to learning disabilities, low test scores, disciplinary problems, grade retentions, or other learning-related factors that could adversely affect the educational performance and attainment of some students. Other terms suggest that an at-risk student is one who requires temporary or ongoing intervention in order to succeed academically and they are less likely to transition successfully into adulthood and achieve economic self-sufficiency.

The label at-risk also suggests that the characteristics of at-risk students include emotional or behavioral problems, truancy, and low academic performance, showing a lack of interest for academics, and expressing a disconnection from the school environment.

Dr. Pooler, challenges these negative terms and labels placed on students and suggest that the characteristics aforementioned provide excuses to lower the bar of expectations for students who are "at potential" of achieving the opposite of negative depictions. This workbook will defy these terms of negativity and propose that youth identified as "at-risk" rip off the labels that has been placed upon you and replace it with "at-potential".

I know that you have the potential of being self-sufficient, getting a higher education and being productive citizens in society when given resources and opportunities to do so.

SO ARE YOU AT-RISK OR AT-POTENTIAL?

Note: This workbook compliments the book: The Cards of Life; when all hope is gone, trust then believe.
By: Dr. Erica Pooler

The Brick Factor (Chapter 1: The Cards of Life -Hell before 5)

• *Self-Identity- Do you know who you are?*

_____
_____
_____
_____
_____
_____

• Who am I?

_____
_____
_____
_____
_____
_____

• What do I stand for?

_____
_____
_____
_____
_____
_____

• What will make you happy?

_____
_____
_____
_____
_____
_____
_____

EVERYBODY HAS A STORY...

I wanted to give up on myself... I wanted to give up on life.

I was a sophomore in College, 14 hours away from home. I went to University of Iowa and lived in GA. I received an academic and sports scholarship for track but around this time I was going on my second hip surgery because of another track injury. I had two surgeries in the same year, one on each hip. I was so down because I had never got a chance to run since I had been in college. I had always been a student-athlete and the fact that I wasn't able to run was emotionally taking a toile on me.

My boyfriend had just broken up with me the day I left for college after Christmas break. He was literally one of my best friends. I had the whole plane ride to think about what had just happened.

Once I got back to Iowa I realized just how much I missed being home. (I am a family type of girl). My family and I are like best friends. One day, as I was sitting in my apartment alone, I let my depression get the best of me. I grabbed a knife. (I had cut before but not since I was about 10 years old). It had been 11 years since I ever thought about hurting myself. The knife hit my skin and I watched the blood gently drip onto my pillow. As I was sobbing, I called my mom since I didn't know what else to do. I told her what I had done and she expressed to me that I needed to go see the on-campus counselor. Instantly, I didn't want to, so I just cleaned up the bloody spatters and went to track practice. To my surprise, my mom flew up to Iowa the next day. She stayed with me for a week and a half and thank God, she did, because I was a broken mess. I thought I could hold it together by myself. Days went by and buckets of tears were shed. I was constantly trembling. We eventually went to see an on-campus counselor, she was not the usual one that I had seen before. She asked me a simple question, "what would make me happy"
Excerpt from: The Cards of Life: Everybody has a story, what's yours?

DR. ERICA FOOLER

CARDS *of* LIFE

POOLER'S POINTS TO PONDER

CARDS *of* LIFE

It is often that parents and educators tend to put labels on students and assume we know the outcome of their life, their path and their story. We look at over achievers and students with high GPA's or star athletes, as if they don't have difficult cards in their lives. EVERYBODY has cards and when we talk about students labeled "At Risk" or as I say "At Potential" we can't assume that they don't have hardships. Oftentimes, we can stereotype students and their circumstances based off of their performance. This young writer is an image of a popular all around good girl with a great future in the eyes of others... But through her lens, she was just as lost and in need of intervention, support, and a listening ear as others that are easier to spot due to their lack of effort, ability or discipline problems. The brick wall of protection is not only masked with misbehavior and disrespect but can also be the straight "A" student, or over achiever with no visible problems at all.

The Brick Factor

• Many students build up a brick wall of protection around them. How high have you built your brick wall of protection? What and who are you protecting yourself from?

_____

_____

_____

_____

_____

_____

• Can you let down your guard just a little to allow others to help you? What does letting your guard down look like to you?

_____

_____

_____

_____

_____

_____

• How do you go through life's many struggles and still become successful?

_____

_____

_____

_____

_____

_____

• What skills are important to you in life in order to be successful and why?

_____

_____

_____

_____

_____

_____

_____

_____

_____

_____

_____

_____

Character: The mental and moral qualities distinctive to an individual, (*pg 5 The Cards of Life*).

EVERYBODY HAS A STORY...

Don't bare loads of secrecy, it will weigh you down.

Between the ages of 4 to 10, I was molested or forced to do provocative things by 10 people I encountered in my life. Growing up my parents were very hard working, they worked for every dime they made.

My mom went through a lot when she was growing up so she didn't want me going through that same struggle. She was molested when she was younger and she never wanted me to go through any of that.

My parents were always working so they had to find people to watch me, little did they know the 'trustworthy' people they would leave me with were the ones who took my innocence away from me.

I didn't know at that time the things I was experiencing at such a young age were wrong, I didn't know that it would shape me into the person I am today, I didn't know it would cause an emotional detachment with people I love and I didn't know they were my drastic cards of life.

I never even told my own parents half the things that happened to me when I was younger, part of the reasons being, I didn't know the things being done to me were bad and I didn't want them to know.

Excerpt: "The Cards of Life: Everybody has a story" 2017

CARDS *of* **LIFE**

• You can't keep it all in because this secret is painful…Think about what secrets you need to tell and find a positive outlet.

_____
_____
_____
_____

• It's hard letting go of the past…. What do you need to let go of in your past?

_____
_____
_____
_____

• Do you allow fear to hold you back? What do you fear?

_____
_____
_____
_____

Trust

Can you think of four people that you can trust with certain information or four people that give you sound advice?
Think of a trustworthy person in these areas of your life?

1. Home:

2. School:

3. Community:

4. Friend:

• **_Education_** – The act or process of imparting or acquiring general knowledge, (Pg.16, The Cards of Life; when all hope is gone, trust then believe 2012).
Is education important to you? Why or Why not?

_____
_____
_____
_____

Your education will make you stand apart. What you know propels you forward in a positive direction.

• **_Sacrifice_** – To surrender something. Sometimes to get to where you want to be you have to give up something or someone. What do you need to give up to reach to your goals? Who do you need to walk away from to meet your goals?

_____
_____
_____
_____

• **_Discipline_** – Training to ensure proper behavior. What is self-discipline?

_____
_____
_____
_____

• **_Humility_** – To be humble and grateful. What or who can you be more grateful for in your life?

_____
_____
_____
_____

• **_Wisdom_** – Plain old good sense. Why is common sense important? What is the difference between book smart and common sense?

_____
_____
_____
_____

• ***Encouragement*** – support, inspiration, hope and courage. Who has your back? What are some things that hold you back from being your best?

1.

2.

3.

4.

•***Excuses***: To give reasons why we can't do something, let's stop making excuses! What would happen, if you didn't allow anything or anyone to stand in the way of your success?

_____
_____
_____
_____
_____
_____

Moving Forward: What is something you can do to continue to move forward?

_____
_____
_____
_____
_____
_____

A Mother is supposed to be there!

As a child, I always thought about how life would be when I got older. My life began to rapidly change for the worst at the age of 5 years old. I was placed in foster care and separated from my mother. There were days when I felt so lonely and I longed for her love. I longed to truly get to know her.

I had to grow up fast as I was exposed to a lot of experiences that I shouldn't have known at five years old. I love my mother with all my heart but there were times that she was not there for me and it was very hard living without her. I felt no one could love me like my mother. There's something about a mother's love, her touch, her voice, the look she gives you, or her smile that is simply irreplaceable. Not having her in my life the way I felt I needed her impacted me on every end. I had to learn how to positively move forward and stop blaming my cards of life on what and who was missing in my world.

Excerpt: "The Cards of Life: Everybody has a story" 2017

CARDS *of* LIFE

POOLER'S POINTS TO PONDER....

CARDS of LIFE

So many children blame their failures on their parents. Yes, it is messed up that we don't all come from the perfect family. Unfortunately, some of us have to grow up fast and the hard way. Not having great parents will make your childhood very tough. Fortunately, you have a choice! You can choose to do great in spite of them or you can make excuses and blame your family and circumstances for your failures. Sometimes we have to just pick up our cards, even when they suck and keep playing our hand.

The BRICK FACTOR (CHAPTER 2: THE CARDS OF LIFE; WHEN ALL HOPE IS GONE- STABILITY)

What is stability?

_____
_____
_____
_____

What makes you feel stable?

_____
_____
_____
_____

What do you like about your neighborhood?

_____
_____
_____
_____

What would you change about your neighborhood?

_____
_____
_____
_____

Who makes up your stable household?

_____
_____
_____
_____

What do you do to support your caregivers and siblings?

_____
_____
_____
_____

Thinking back, everyone has a saying that parents give you as advice... What is a saying that you can live by...What stands out that makes you remember this?
Ex: "What goes on in this house, stays in this house."

EVERYBODY HAS A STORY...

When Parents are put in Prison it ruins families...

As a baby, my father went to prison for robbing a bank and he served seven years. When he got out of prison I was eight years old. He stayed in my life for three years and yes indeed, these three years felt like ten! Within those three years, he gave me the world and explained the way he made it happen. He would stress to me, "this is not the life you want" It took me a while to get it but eventually I did. My family consisted of my mom, sister, my dad and myself. After three years of the good life, my world again fell apart. I found myself in a devastating situation and my mom and dad were taken from me… Yet again I lost my dad to the prison system as he was sentenced for selling drugs. My mom fell apart and just could not handle the pressure.

My family had to move to Alabama which is what really shaped who I am. My mom's side of the family lived there but I barely knew them. We moved into a trailer and my life continued in a downward spiral from there. This trailer had doors hanging off the hinges, trees growing from under it and the dilapidated conditions were unbearable. I believe it was at this point my mom gave up basically throwing in the towel to fight for our family to get back on our feet. This is when her problems and pressures fell onto my sister and I. I think this is when I became a man, as I had to assume the role. To me this was impossible. My sister and I had to move around from one family member to another. We had no clue as to what would happen next to us. We hoped that we could stay together and not be separated. It seemed like all we had was each other. This reality came to a halt when my sisters' dad came and took her back to Florida after learning about our living conditions and struggles that we were going through. I had the option to go but chose to stay because I love my mom. I was worried about her and did not want to leave her alone. I thought I could help and support her to quit her alcoholic addiction. That's what I thought…

Excerpt: "The Cards of Life: Everybody has a story" 2017

CARDS *of* LIFE

Describe a time when you wanted to give up and why?

_____

_____

_____

_____

_____

_____

_____

_____

_____

_____

_____

When you want to give up, what keeps you going?

_____

_____

_____

_____

_____

_____

_____

_____

_____

_____

_____

_____

How can you grow from your life challenges?

_____

_____

_____

_____

_____

_____

_____

_____

_____

_____

_____

How do you overcome the pain of your past?

_____
_____
_____
_____
_____
_____
_____
_____
_____
_____
_____

How can you create your own success?

_____
_____
_____
_____
_____
_____
_____
_____
_____
_____
_____
_____
_____
_____
_____
_____
_____
_____
_____
_____

Generational Curses - taking away innocence.

Growing up my parents always wanted to keep me away from harm and danger, believing that every person that encountered my life wouldn't have the power to hurt me in any way. It's the people that you least expect to do any harm towards your child that end up causing the most pain and hurt. The people they least expected to ever do any wrong to me was family. Yes, so-called "family". The ones who are supposed to care for my well-being, love me unconditionally and never hurt me in any way, shape or form.

My past continued to propel my future, I was in a relationship once where I struggled to open up, share how I felt, and be completely vulnerable. I could never truly love him because I was so guarded and protective of my heart, mind, body, and soul. It was to the point where I felt uncomfortable when he touched me or even a simple embrace or innocent kiss. Something just rubbed me the wrong way so I pushed him further and further away. I pushed someone who gave me unconditional love, someone who was trustworthy, and someone who truly cared about my well-being away. All because of my baggage that I never let go of. He'd always ask me "why? Why do you push me away?" And I'd just say I don't know when deep down I knew... I knew why I was so guarded and why I felt so uncomfortable around someone who is supposed to love me. I had this mindset of, well if my own blood could hurt me, so could you, but he never hurt me. Ultimately, I destroyed my relationship. I know first-hand how hard it is to forgive someone. I've cried many nights until my pillow was drenched in tears. I deeply understand disappointment, pain, and struggling to forgive myself and the people who hurt me. But I now know that walking around angry and bitter about who has hurt me causes me to live a miserable and negative life. As long as you are bitter and negative you will repeal happiness and peace in your life.

I've always wondered why it was so hard for me to attach to people and connect with someone physically and emotionally. I've always wondered why it's so hard for me to trust people. Looking back, I now realize why I am the way I am. I now realize why trusting people isn't easy for me but I can't shut everyone out. It's hard for me to accept people into my life because for so long I never dealt with my past and what I went through as a child.
Excerpt: "The Cards of Life: Everybody has a story" 2017

19

Everyday life will present you with an obstacle and it will be up you to assert your worth, uplift yourself to keep going and have faith you will make it. – Dr. Erica Pooler

When you know, understand and accept your past, it can drastically help you in steer your path to a better future.

What do you know about your past ancestors and family members? What "runs in" your family?

_____
_____
_____
_____

Do you have generational curses that you must overcome in your family?

_____
_____
_____
_____

Key terms:
(pg. 16, The Cards of Life; when all hope is gone) **Education** – the act of imparting general knowledge, developing reasoning, judgment, and preparing intellectually for a mature life.
Are you progressing with your education the way you would like to?

What are your strengths and weaknesses?

Sacrifice – The surrendering or giving up of something for the sake of something desired.
What sacrifices do you need to make to become a better you?

_____
_____
_____
_____

Discipline – Training to ensure proper behavior and enforcing acceptable patterns of behavior.
Who disciplines you?

Why?

And How?

At this point in your life you need to be working on self-discipline...
What does self-discipline mean to you?

_____

_____

_____

_____

Wisdom – the quality of having experience, knowledge, and good judgment; the quality of being wise. (Webster Dictionary)

Who do you consider a wise person and why?

_____

_____

_____

_____

Do you make wise decisions? Why or Why not?

_____

_____

_____

_____

What can you do to ensure good judgment on your part?

_____

_____

_____

_____

When you don't fit...

> "Baby remember, everyone else is here because they can afford to be here, you are here because they want you here."
> Those were the words my mother would say to me every day as we drove an hour from Opa-Locka, Florida, to my school that cost roughly twenty-three thousand dollars a year. That school was the first of the several schools whose tuitions would exceed my mother's yearly income. It was also the first of many that would make me feel out of place at times.
>
> I never thought much about the fact my mother drove all the way back to go to work, only that my car was not a Range Rover or a brand-new Benz. I was young and I wouldn't come to understand how valuable a working car was until I moved away for college. But, during that time, I hated safety patrols because the kids would walk up to my car and help me out. Why was I so ashamed to be helped? It didn't help that they called my car the "AIDS" car because the paint job was rusting. In fact, nothing ever helped. I loved uniforms because I didn't have to think about what I wore and if my clothes were name brand. For a very long time I felt I just didn't fit.
> Excerpt: "The Cards of Life: Everybody has a story" 2017

The sooner you realize that you are ultimately in charge of how you value life and start placing personal investments in yourself, the further you will get.

Humility – the quality or state of not thinking you are better than other people: the quality or state of being humble.

Why are these attributes (education, discipline, sacrifice, and humility) important in life?

_____
_____
_____
_____
_____
_____
_____
_____
_____
_____
_____
_____

Rate 1-4. 1 being the most important and 4 being the least in YOU being successful and why?

Education

Wisdom

Humility

Sacrifice

23

Education should always be joined to your goals as it will always make you stand apart. What you know will propel you in every decision and it can save you from a lifetime of struggle, heartache, and pain when accompanied by a bit of common sense.

• Time Management – Get your priorities in check. "Time waits for no man." Where does the time go?

How much time do you invest in your future?

_____
_____
_____
_____
_____
_____
_____
_____
_____
_____
_____
_____

When you enter middle school and high school, usually you are excited! When entering a new school for the first time, you have a clean slate; an opportunity to start over and begin fresh; An opportunity to right your wrongs.
Usually is used loosely if you are already in an alternative school or an incarcerated youth. This type of trouble and record may follow you. You will have to work hard to prove them wrong (naysayers – people who don't believe in you or think you won't amount to anything).
There will be a great deal of time invested in getting a solid education or a great deal of time wasted. It is imperative to invest time in yourself, education and future. Remember, what you put in is what you get out.

Translation – garbage in; garbage out.

This begins with the music you listen to, the food you eat, to the lack of intellectual stimulation such as reading, writing/reflecting and most importantly the people you entertain and your self-worth/respect.

Practice makes you better (nobody is perfect) – you may hate to read because you struggle, or you don't like math because it's confusing or you are too far behind…but, doing nothing to get better, doesn't help your situation.

Daddy Issues led to Baby Daddy issues,

"My mom and I never had that mother-daughter bond where I could sit and tell her everything I felt inside. As I grew, it just got hard to let my feelings out. Moving into a new environment being told not to call or write daddy from our new address. Do you know how hard that was? Someone you love to death. I stayed in the house with no friends. It was just my only sister. She is a year above my age group so she grew up a little bit faster than me. She started clubbing, got a boyfriend and you know everything else that follows that!! She was still my diary though, but eventually, my trust became very low so I started keeping to myself.

As time progressed, I met a boy that I fell head over heels with. He became everything I felt I was lacking. Soon after I was pregnant with my first son at 16 and pregnant with twins a year later. That boy never grew into a man and what I thought was going to be forever, a relationship of love turned into bitter hate. So, I now have three kids who are the love of my life and lord knows it's not easy but they give me a reason to fight. They give me a reason to keep pushing. I have learned to be independent and do what I have to do to provide a better life. My advice to you would be to finish school and don't get caught up in the boys because they will sell you a false dream. The female is generally left picking up the pieces. So when he says he loves you and will always be there. Do you believe him?"

Excerpt: "The Cards of Life: Everybody has a story" 2017

EVERYBODY HAS A STORY...

Being bullied turned me into someone else?

Unlike most high school students, I wasn't your typical black kid, I was always the oddball of the groups, I was a loner at heart and wasn't one to join in the crowd to fit in. This social awkwardness had a major impact on my high school life and during my years in high school, I struggled with depression, social anxiety, bullying, anger issues and being classified as "At- Risk" unable to finish college.

In high school, bullying was the main obstacle that I struggled with and due to the fact that I wasn't social, it was hard to explain to those around me how I felt. I constantly worried about being judged and the fear of being labeled. Unbeknownst to me, being quiet and isolated about issues I was going through only made things worse. I was young and overtime I began to cut people out of my life that really mattered to me, such as, family and close friends. People didn't understand that bullying caused my mind to become alert to the wrong things and took my thoughts away from my current reality. When that mindset was in place it caused me to believe that I was not capable of accomplishing certain things. I began to see people differently, I began to treat those who once cared about me further away. Suddenly I realized that I had a sense of lost identity but in reality, I was doing it to myself.

From my own personal experience, it cost me time, money, and almost got my expelled from school. Bullying turned me into someone else I became mean, aggressive and even somewhat lost hope and had no regard for my life. When I got to that point I wrote a letter to a close friend expressing my feelings and I was eventually sent to a rehab center where I finally got my mind right. I soon realized that there's a lot to depression. This feeling added on to the issues I already had. When those around me made fun of me "for simply being me" It caused me more issues that needed to be dealt with on daily bases.

Bullying was a huge road block for me that almost took me out! Don't allow obstacles to block you from being your best. Find a way to positively play your hand to the best of your ability.
Excerpt: "The Cards of Life: Everybody has a story" 2018

Pooler's Points to Ponder...

CARDS of LIFE

It's never too late to work on building positive relationships with your parents or a responsible adult, in the end it can save you a lot of heartache and looking for love in all the wrong places.

After school is out you have to do a little bit more...

How much time do you spend?

Reading	
Listening to Music	
Watching Television	
Writing	
Playing with Technology	
Talking	
Sports	
Sleep	

Calculate and think about the minutes per week spent on the table above.

Calculate and think about the hours per week spent on the table above.

Calculate and think about the days per week spent on the table above.

Days per week

Think about where you invest your time and energy daily, monthly and yearly.

What would happen if you aligned your actions with your purpose and passion?

Think about your goals and review the aforementioned data on where you are spending your time. Work on getting your goals to align with your actions.

"Whether you think you can or you can't, your right!"- Henry Ford

1. Short Term Goals (up to 6 months) Be detailed	
2. Action Steps/Lists What you can do right now?	
3. Overcoming Road Blocks *Plan to go around barriers and naysayers*	

How will you measure these short-term goals?

_____
_____
_____
_____
_____
_____

How will you hold yourself accountable for reaching these goals?

_____
_____
_____
_____
_____
_____

How often will you review your progress on these short-term goals?

_____
_____
_____
_____
_____
_____

Describe how you will feel once these short-term goals are met.

_____
_____
_____
_____
_____
_____

What is your deepest fear?

_____
_____
_____
_____
_____
_____

Do you want to be successful?

_____
_____
_____
_____
_____
_____

What are you willing to do to ensure that success is in your future?

_____
_____
_____
_____
_____
_____

Never apologize for being who you are! If you struggle with bullying and depression find someone that you can trust and talk about your options. Don't be defeated by this card!

Goals and proven facts…

Did you know that people who commit their goals to paper are 50% more likely to achieve them than people who do not?

Did you know that only 3 of every 100 people actually write their goals down?

92% of people who make New Year's Resolutions fail within 15 days…

It's great that we are not in this selected group of non-examples. Think about what you want in life. Think about your goals, dreams and aspirations. What keeps you up at night? What do you think you were placed on this earth to accomplish?

_____
_____
_____
_____
_____
_____

A **short-term goal** is defined as something you want to do in the near future. The near future can mean today, this week, this month, or even this year. A **short-term goal** is something you want to accomplish soon. You may have many short-term goals to reach your long-term goals.

Long Term Goals – A long term goal is also a committed list or plan for personal or professional accomplishments, the time frame is more than 6 months to a few years.

How will you measure these short and long-term goals?

_____
_____
_____
_____
_____
_____

How will you hold yourself accountable for reaching these goals?

_____
_____
_____
_____
_____
_____

How often will you review your progress on these short and long-term goals?

_____
_____
_____
_____
_____
_____

Some of these questions you may have to come back to after putting in the work over time

Have you met your short-term goals yet? If so which ones.

_____
_____
_____
_____

What was the hardest part of sticking to your short-term goals and list?

_____

_____

_____

_____

Did the anticipated road blocks become a problem?

_____

_____

_____

_____

Did you follow through on overcoming negativity and naysayers?

_____

_____

_____

_____

Describe how you will feel once these long-term goals are met.

_____

_____

_____

_____

Whenever you are trying to do something positive, you will certainly face obstacles, you must persevere and be able to bare difficulties and be steadfast despite how many challenges come your way. I have worked with the most "at risk" students from all walks of life, living out of their cars working two jobs to help their parents take care of their siblings. Gang bangers, addicts, I even had students' "shot at" in their neighborhoods, running with the wrong crowds and they simply don't know how to get back on the right track. Yet they come to school, because it's their only hope. Some have yet to learn that life doesn't accept excuses and education is their key to freedom. Now is the time to get it together! No matter where you are or which wrong road you have traveled: school, alternative education, juvenile, or level program; its time out for excuses.

Today you choose which path you're going to take. Once you hit bottom, you can go nowhere but up. You must believe that you can accomplish great things, connect with positive people who can guide you down the right path and expect wonderful things out of your life. Break down your brick walls and discover what's on the inside of you.

CARDS *of* LIFE

Everyone was put on this earth for something...

What do you think you were put on this earth for and why?

_____
_____
_____
_____
_____
_____
_____
_____
_____

What do you think your purpose is and why?

_____
_____
_____
_____
_____
_____
_____
_____

What can be done to help you reach your full potential?

_____
_____
_____
_____
_____
_____
_____
_____
_____

EVERYBODY HAS A STORY...

Arrested for Robbery.

I have always been a class clown because it was something that I was good at and people liked me because of this, I personally liked all the attention. Since I chose to be a class clown that led to me getting in trouble in school. I was receiving after school detentions, in and out of school suspensions.

In 2008, my mom and step dad decided that they were going to get a divorce. When they did this, I was hurt and surprised, like my step dad was the only dad I knew. My mom, my younger brother, and I were moving to Orlando. I had never lived anywhere but in Brevard County before and did not know anyone. School started up and I started making friends by being a class clown. However, being a class clown led to me receiving referrals, and I started hanging with the wrong crowd. I felt like I had to impress them so I started falling into their peer pressure, this consisted of skipping school, smoking weed, drinking underage, and taking prescription pills. I was only in the 7th grade at this time. Then one day my best friend wanted some money and I agreed that some money would be nice. Therefore, we broke into our middle school. We stole money after school that Friday. We took dumb stuff like candy and a lockbox.

Well Monday came around and my friends were bragging about what we did Friday soon enough the rumor found its way to the dean's office. While I was in class there was a knock at the door then my dean Mr. Durias, the resource deputy and two detectives pulled me out of class. Mr. Durias told me that they had some questions for me. Then he left the two detectives and me in his office. One of the detectives closed the door while the other detective placed a tape recorder on the desk he then introduced himself and his partner did the same. The next thing they did was read me my rights. I waived them because I was not sure what they were going to ask me. Well they brought up that the school had a break in Friday evening. I acted as if I had no idea about a burglary. They left the room and closed the door. Well they soon returned about 15 minutes later, when they did there was someone else with them, it was my MOM. The detectives explained why I was up there, they then asked me to stand up and turn around, and proceeded to tell my mom and I that I was under arrest for burglary and felony criminal mischief.
Excerpt: "The Cards of Life: Everybody has a story" 2018

A WRONG DECISION CAN DERAIL YOUR LIFE, BUT IT'S NEVER TOO LATE TO GET BACK ON THE RIGHT TRACK!

Making dumb decisions can send your life in a downward spiral that can be so difficult to turn it around. In society today, even when you do turn it around it can be too late.

What's a decision you made in life that you regret?

Was it hard to overcome that hardship?

Don't allow your past to block your path to being successful
    – Dr. Erica Pooler

What are 3 things you can do to turn your DREAM into REALITY?

1.

_____
_____
_____
_____
_____

2.

_____
_____
_____
_____
_____

3.

_____
_____
_____
_____
_____

"You have no control over the cards that are dealt to you in life, but it's up to you as to how the game is played." – Dr. Erica Pooler

What is your definition of **Success**?

_____
_____
_____
_____
_____

What are 3 **strengths** you possess?

1.

_____
_____
_____
_____
_____

2.

_____
_____
_____
_____
_____

3.

_____
_____
_____
_____
_____

How will you use YOUR strengths to attain your success?

_____
_____
_____
_____
_____

How can you improve in these areas to increase YOUR chance of attaining success?

Knowledge	
Confidence	
Presence	
Self-Discipline	

Keeping Your Eyes on the Prize

Dedication: What does it mean to you?

_____
_____
_____
_____

• **Future Effects:** What or who are you dedicated to?

_____
_____
_____
_____

• **Determination:** What does it mean to you?

_____
_____
_____
_____

• What things do you have to overcome?

_____
_____
_____
_____

• **Discipline:** What does it mean to you?

_____
_____
_____
_____

• What storms are you pushing through (don't give up keep pushing)?

_____
_____
_____
_____

"I AM"

I am or once was broken to the very core of my existence. A product of my environment a vast makeup of my upbringing; my past defined and restrained me like brick walls blocking my path and impeding my success. Statistics had me bound by clarifying the road that I would take

Blaming was my agenda and making excuses to fail was my story. The ability to press forward with the weight of the world dragging behind me was a burden I couldn't carry alone. The ability to breathe when I no longer wanted to live was also out of my control.

There was always a bigger plan that I could never explain, my cards of life were too drastic to maintain.

There was a feeling of fear in the pit of my stomach, accompanied the whisper in my ear that said it would get better. The pierce in my heart when the unthinkable became my reality, when my loved ones took their last breath my world completely fell apart.

At a distinctive point in my life, the power of "I am" for me was redefined. It turned my Negative outlook to positive overcoming. My I can't attitude to slightly removed the "T"
My "I won't" humbled itself into submission, my brick walls shattered.

Wisdom imparted from the pain and sorrow, I gave charge to the power that I held within. Choosing to no longer be bound by my circumstances. I discovered there is power that lies in me, my tongue helped me to change the words that follow "I am"
And therefore, my actions aligned and gave away to my destiny

Enabling me to persevere. Despite difficulties, failure, or opposition-- I chose to press. I refuse to quit, I am determined to not allow my life circumstances to dictate how I play my cards.

So, who am I?

I am who I say I am

By: Dr. Erica Pooler

Poem Reflection:

_____
_____
_____
_____
_____
_____
_____
_____
_____
_____
_____
_____
_____
_____
_____

WHAT IF?

What if we knew the real you?
What if you could dig into the deepest part of your being, shed the layers of
doubt, fear and uncertainty?
Unlock your deepest secret and allow healing from all your pain?
If you could turn back time, what would you erase?
What if you truly learned how much you could bring to the world?
If you encouraged and motivated one another rather than bringing each
other down?
If you could understand your beauty, worth your value,
Identify your purpose, your destiny and reason for existence.
What if you didn't care about what other people thought because you were
being true to yourself?

If the views of society, politics, or popularity didn't matter
If you could bounce off negativity unkind words and names unbecoming of
you,
What if you could allow light to pierce your soul and not be blinded by
judgment or hatred?

What if you could not fail, if you did not allow fear to paralyze you, your thoughts and actions? What if you stopped making excuses to fail and used your circumstances as a reason to succeed. If you lowered your brick walls of protection and allowed people to help you because everyone is not here to hurt you.
What if you stopped making excuses to fail and use your circumstances as a reason to succeed.
What if you made sacrifices and persevered through every storm?
If you never gave up on your dreams and never surrendered your passion! What if you never quit?

What if?

By: Dr. Erica Pooler

Poem Reflection:

_____
_____
_____
_____
_____
_____
_____
_____

Compare and contrast the two poems "I am" and "What if"
How are they alike and different? Does either poem resonate with you? Do we know the real you?

Reflection:

_____
_____
_____
_____
_____
_____
_____
_____
_____
_____
_____

What was the author's message or point of view in the poems?

_____
_____
_____
_____
_____
_____

What is your mission, dream, or passion?

_____
_____
_____
_____
_____
_____

What do you want to accomplish in your life?

_____
_____
_____
_____
_____
_____

What is your "I AM"? Affirm yourself?

_____
_____
_____
_____
_____
_____

What do you need to change about you?

_____
_____
_____
_____
_____
_____

"What if" you never gave up on your dreams?

_____
_____
_____
_____
_____
_____

What would your future look like?

_____
_____
_____
_____
_____

Life deals us many cards…. But you must continue the game and never give up!

What will you do with the hands you have been dealt?

_____
_____
_____
_____
_____
_____
_____
_____
_____
_____
_____

Know that in life you will be dealt many cards. You may want to throw your hand in the deck or simply give up. But take it from me. If you do you will never see your true potential. You may never know how great you could be. Your future will be better than your past. Even if you lose your way, make several mistakes and drift on your journey of life; you can always find your way back on the right side of the tracks. Continue to grow daily, move forward and be the very best version of yourself that you can be; especially when no one is watching. In life, you will make mistakes but hope is not lost, trust and believe in yourself. I certainly believe in you.

Dr. Erica Pooler

A special thanks to a few of my young contributors to this workbook who learned to play their hands in the cards of life. A small portion of their stories are featured in this workbook in hopes that you can gain something from their past troubles. They will be featured in the book: The Cards of Life: Everybody has a story what's yours?

Know that you are not alone and tragedies, unfavorable cards in life, and obstacles affect us all. It doesn't discriminate and there's no bias. However, if you stay the course and never give up, I promise you success will follow.

I am very proud of "My Cards of Life Teens" who are now Adults. As I always say, once a Pooler kid, always a Pooler kid.

Mikeia Pooler
Amir Begali
Jonathan Bertrand
Kiebriana Alshabazz
Sylicia McKenzie
Chris Cobb
Da'quesha Irvin
Shannen Rose Ford

NOTES_____

_____
_____
_____
_____
_____
_____
_____
_____
_____
_____
_____
_____
_____
_____
_____
_____
_____
_____
_____
_____
_____
_____
_____
_____
_____
_____
_____
_____
_____
_____
_____
_____
_____
_____
_____
_____
_____

NOTES_____

_____

_____

_____

_____

_____

_____

_____

_____

_____

_____

_____

_____

_____

_____

_____

_____

_____

_____

_____

_____

_____

_____

_____

_____

_____

_____

_____

_____

_____

_____

_____

_____

_____

_____

_____

_____

_____

_____

Made in the USA
Monee, IL
04 January 2023

24476314R00032